Bear Cub

Bear Cub

Written by Sarah Toast

Illustrated by Krista Brauckmann-Towns

Publications International, Ltd.

As summer draws to an end, Mother Bear roams through the mountain forest. She gathers and eats enormous amounts of berries and fruit.

Mother Bear puts on fat so she can sleep through the winter. The layer of fat will keep her warm. It will help her provide milk for the baby bear that will be born, too.

Mother Bear chooses a rocky cave to be her den. She will stay in the den during the winter. It will protect her from the cold wind and blowing snow. Mother Bear pads it with moss, leaves, and grass. She makes it warm and soft for herself and the baby.

As snow begins to fall, Mother Bear settles down to sleep.

In the middle of winter, snow drifts are deep outside the den. Mother Bear's tiny cub is born. His eyes are closed. He has hardly any fur. The cub will grow quickly, nourished by Mother Bear's milk.

Mother Bear and Baby Bear continue to sleep. Mother Bear will wake up and protect Baby Bear if the den is disturbed.

In a few weeks Baby Bear's eyes open. He is now covered in thick, soft fur. Mother Bear and Baby Bear stay in their snug den another month.

In the spring Baby Bear and his mother emerge from the den. Mother Bear shows Baby Bear how to look for food. She shows him the tender shoots that make a good meal.

Mother Bear makes her way with Baby Bear to the elks' winter range. They walk down a grassy slope. She lifts up her head and sniffs the breeze. Baby Bear raises his head, too. He moves his head back and forth so hard he falls over.

Mother Bear finds an elk that died in the winter. The elk died when the snows were deep and not enough food could be found.

Mother Bear eats what she can of the nourishing elk meat. Then she buries it in a shallow hole. She covers it with leaves, twigs, and dirt. She will return to it later.

Baby Bear learns by watching what his mother does. Baby Bear must learn three important rules. He must follow mother, obey mother, and have fun.

Mother Bear teaches her cub to turn over fallen branches. She shows him how to look for grubs to eat. Baby Bear and Mother Bear dig up bulbs, roots, and snails. They use their long, sharp claws.

When his mother stops to rest, Baby Bear climbs all over her. He somersaults into her lap. He nibbles her ears, then runs off to chase a field mouse.

Mother Bear looks up from playing with her cub. She sees a lean wolf watching them. Quickly, she chases the cub into a hollow tree stump. Then she turns to face the wolf.

Mother Bear stands up on her hind legs. She swings her front paws and growls loudly. The wolf runs away.

Mother Bear calls to her cub. He does not come out of the hollow stump. Mother Bear goes to find out why.

Baby Bear has found a treat. It is a honeycomb with honey from last summer. Baby Bear sticks his little paw into the honeycomb and licks it. He tastes the wildflowers of summer in the sweet honey.

Baby Bear backs out of the hollow log. He brings some tasty honeycomb for his mother. She happily eats the honey. Then she and her cub give each other a true bear hug.

The End